Succeeding with a Notespeller

by Helen Marlais with Cynthia Coster

Production: Frank J. Hackinson
Production Coordinators: Peggy Gallagher and Philip Groeber
Cover and Interior Illustrations: Melissa L. Ballard,
    Las Flores, California
Cover Design: Andi Whitmer
Cover Art Concept: Helen Marlais
Engraving: Tempo Music Press, Inc.
Printer: Tempo Music Press, Inc.

ISBN-13: 978-1-61928-036-6

Table of Contents

FJH2209

Review of Treble Staff Guide Notes

"Hooray . . . It's Fall!"

• Can you find and name all the guide notes?

Review of Bass Staff Guide Notes

"Pumpkin Patch"

• Can you find and name all the guide notes?

FJH2209

Review of Melodic 2nds

"Falling Leaves"

• Draw a 2nd **up** from the given note and name each note.

• Draw a 2nd **down** from the given note and name each note.

Now play each note on the piano.

Review of Melodic 3rds

"Birds of a Feather . . .

• Draw a 3rd **up** from the given note and name each note.

• Draw a 3rd **down** from the given note and name each note.

Now play these notes on the piano.

FJH2209

Review of Melodic 4ths

. . . also Eat Together."

• Draw a 4th **up** from the given note and name each note.

• Draw a 4th **down** from the given note and name each note.

Now play these notes on the piano.

Review of Melodic 5ths

"Soccer Practice"

• Draw an X through the soccer balls that are **NOT** 5ths.

Then play all the melodic 5ths on the piano.

FJH2209

Review of Melodic 6ths
"More Soccer Drills"

• Draw an X through the soccer balls that are **NOT** 6ths.

Then play all
the melodic 6ths
on the piano.

Chocolate Shakes

Harmonic 6ths

"Enjoy a Tasty Treat at . . .

• Draw a harmonic 6th **above** the given note and name each note.

• Draw a harmonic 6th **below** the given note and name each note.

FJH2209

Banana Split

More Melodic Intervals

Hot Fudge Sundae

...an Old-Fashioned Fountain Shop"

• Name the notes and intervals.

G C

4th

"Let's Go Shopping with the C Major Scale"

• Draw and name the notes of the C Scale in each staff.

"Up the C Scale on the Escalator"

• Name each note of the C Scale.

FJH2209

"More Shopping with the C Major Triads"

• Draw and name the notes of the C Major triads in the treble staff.

"Up the C Triad on the Escalator"

• Draw the missing C Major triad notes in each shopping bag.

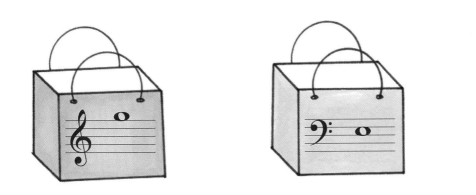

• Draw and name the notes of each C Major triad below.

"G Scale Surprise for You!"

- Draw the missing notes on the staff of each G scale.
- Name each note.

G Major has
1♯ — F♯

G _ _ B _ _ _ G

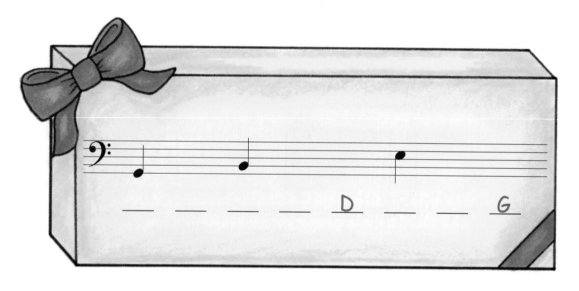

_ _ _ _ D _ _ G

Don't forget
the F♯ in the
G Major scale!

- Draw the missing notes of each G Major scale and name each note.
- Remember the F♯s.

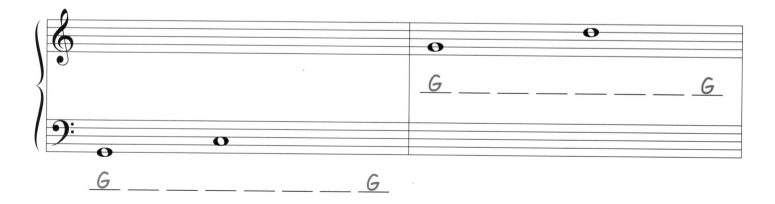

G _ _ _ _ _ _ G

G _ _ _ _ _ _ _ G

FJH2209

"It's a Birthday Party with G Major Triads"

- Name all the notes in the G Major triad in each party hat.

- Draw the missing G Major triad notes in each birthday cake.

- Draw the missing G Major triad notes and name each note.

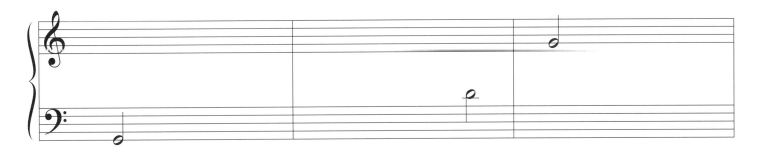

"Snowboarding Down the D Major Scale Slope"

D Major has
2♯s — F♯ and C♯

- Fill in the missing notes of each descending D Major scale.
- Name each note to help the snowboarders reach the finish line.

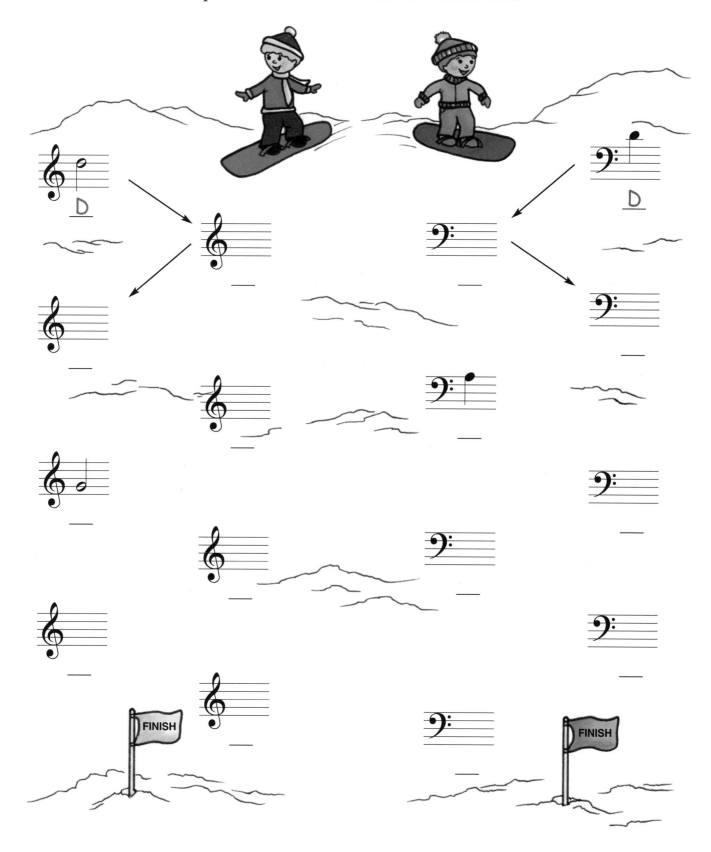

FJH2209

"More Fun on the Slopes"

Draw the D Major triads in each snow mound using D F♯ A as shown in the D Major scales on the previous page.

Bonus: Draw the D Major triad on this treble staff starting with Treble D.

"Let's Work Out with Ledger Line Notes Above the Bass Staff C-D-E"

• Name or draw the notes in each piece of equipment.

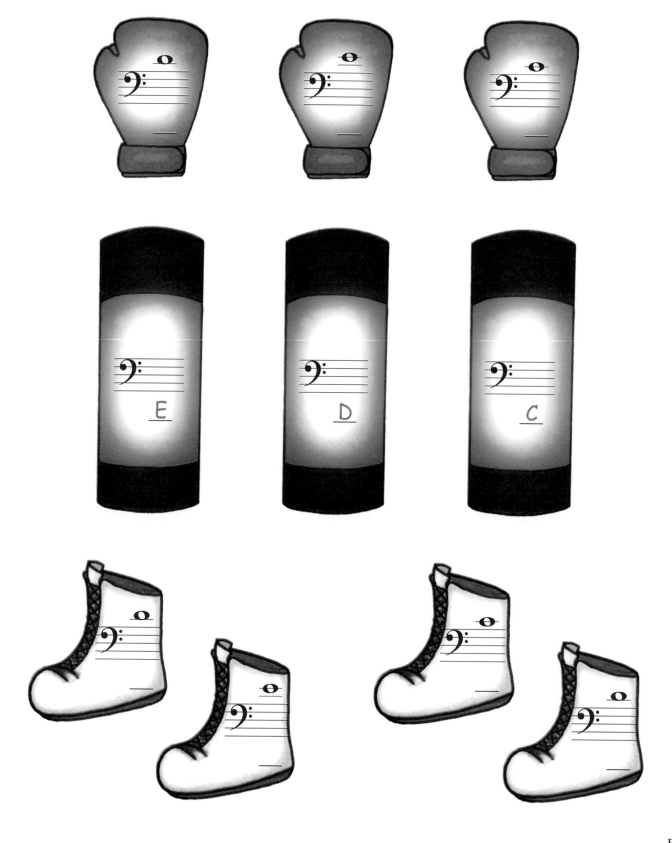

"Exercising the Brain"

• Put an X through the incorrect dumbbells.

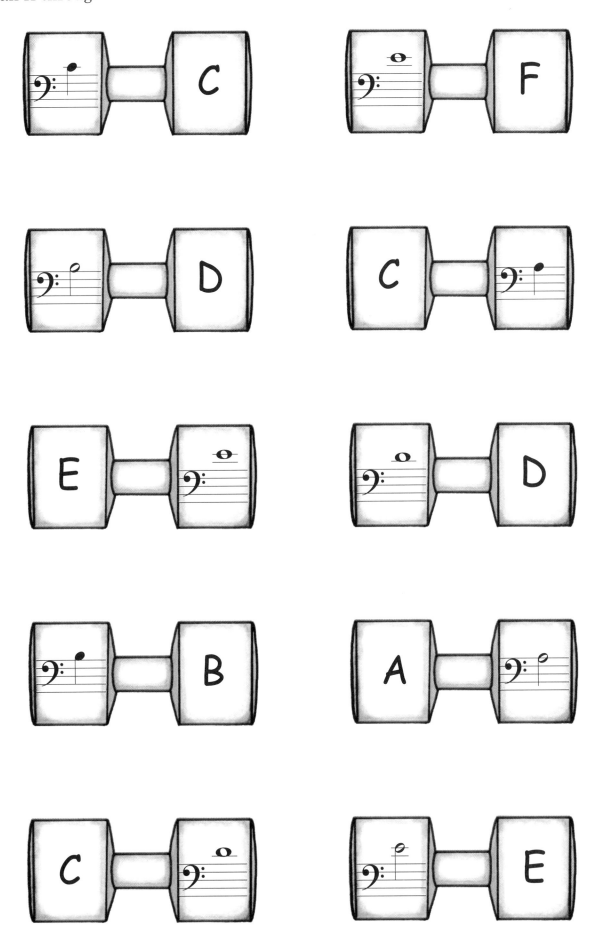

"A Rain Forest Adventure"

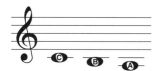

• Name the notes. Then play the notes.

• Name the notes. Then play the notes.

Ledger Line Notes Above the Treble Staff

· Name each guide note.

· Name each treble ledger note.

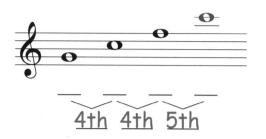

4th 4th 5th

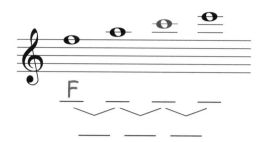

F

Bonus: Each ledger note is a _____ apart.
Circle the correct answer:
2nd   3rd   4th

"Diving for Clams"

· Name the notes and intervals.

"Dodging Sharks and Octopus as We Dive for Clams"

• Name the notes and intervals.

Ledger Line Notes Above the Treble Staff

"Higher and Higher We Go"

- Name each note in the windows as she rappels up the building.

- Draw the treble ledger notes in each rappelling hard hat.

FJH2209

F - A - C - E

- Draw the treble ledger notes in each window
  as the girl rappels down the 4-story building.

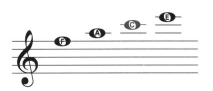

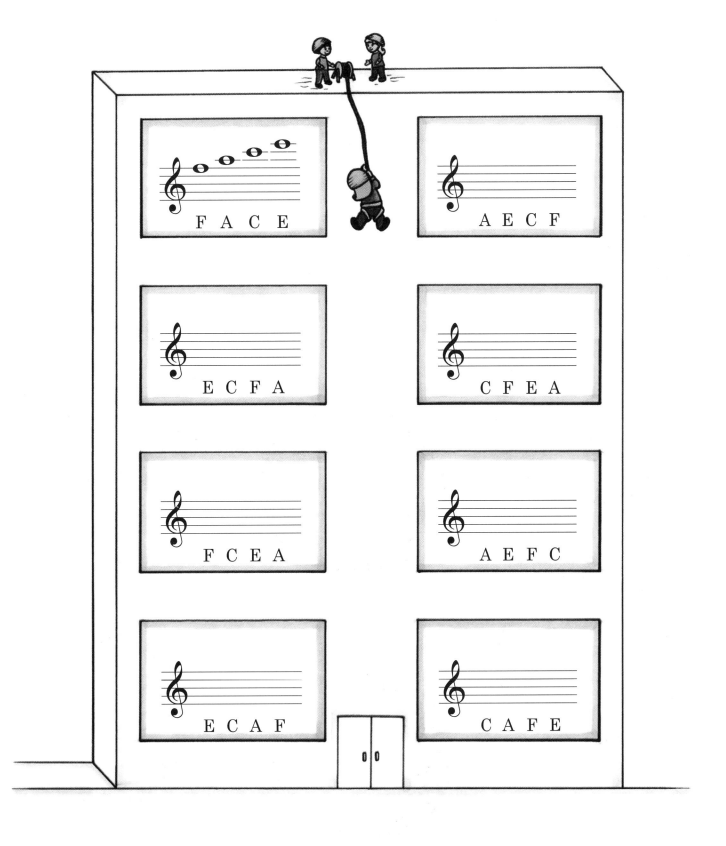

F A C E

A E C F

E C F A

C F E A

F C E A

A E F C

E C A F

C A F E

Ledger Line Notes Below the Bass Staff

• Name each guide note.

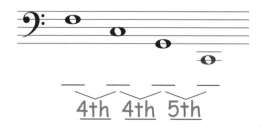

4th 4th 5th

• Name each bass ledger line note.

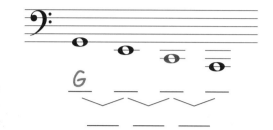

G

Bonus: Each ledger line note is a _____ apart. Circle the correct answer:
2nd   3rd   4th

"Marching to the Beat of the Bass Drum"

• Name the notes and interval in each bass drum. Then play each note.

FJH2209

"Let's Keep Marching"

· Draw the notes in each bass drum using bass ledger notes.

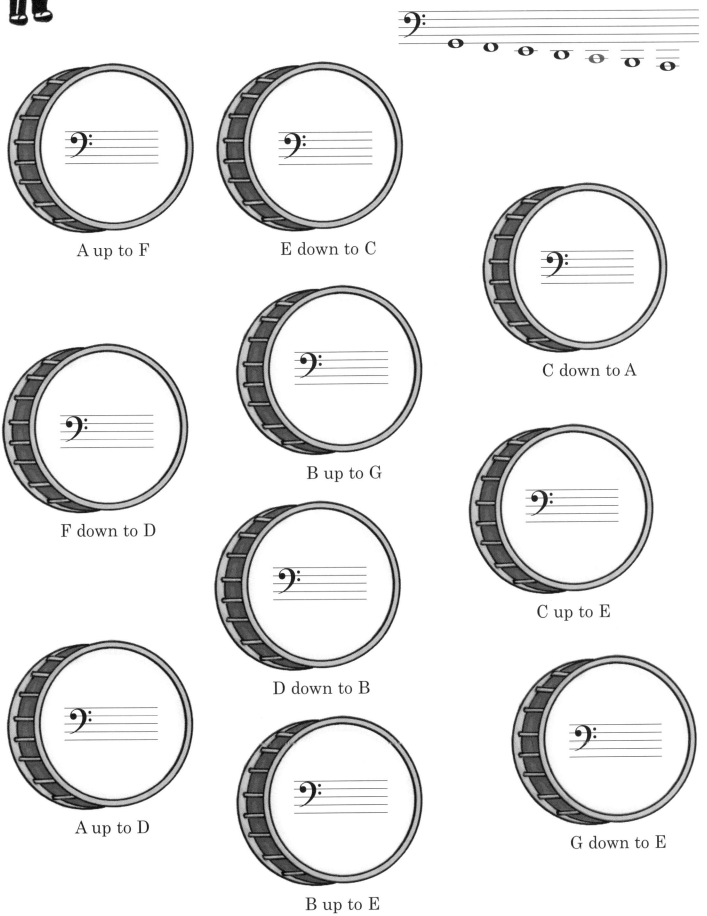

A up to F

E down to C

C down to A

B up to G

F down to D

D down to B

C up to E

A up to D

G down to E

B up to E

Ledger Line Notes Below the Bass Staff

"Bailing Hay . . .

• Name the notes and interval in each tractor.

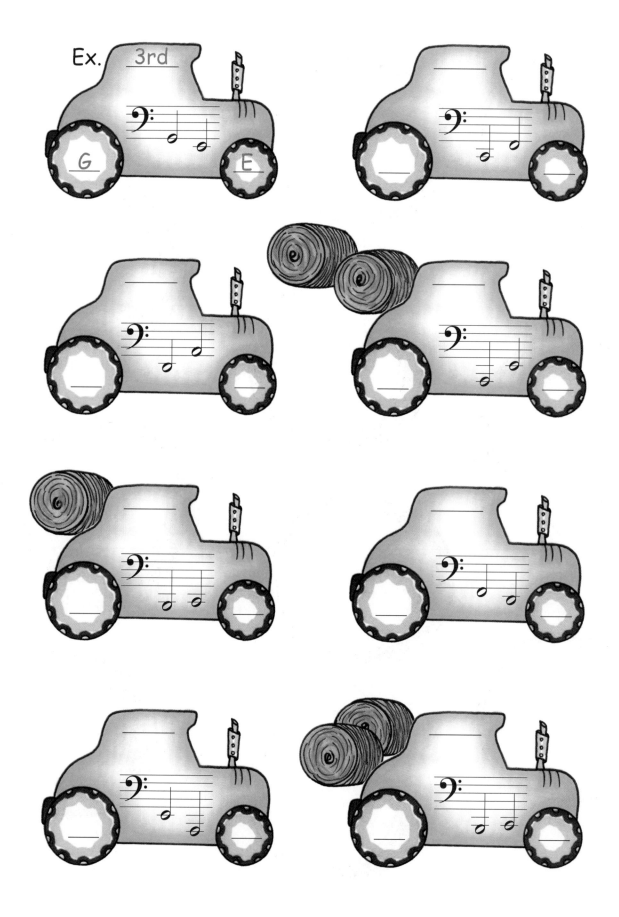

. . . on the Farm"

• Put an X through the bales of hay that are incorrect.

Then play all the correct notes.

"Test Your Tae Kwon Do Skills with the A Major Scale"

• Earn each belt by naming and drawing the missing notes in each A Major scale and A Major triad. Remember the 3 sharps!

A Major has 3♯s — F♯, C♯, and G♯.

A Major Scale

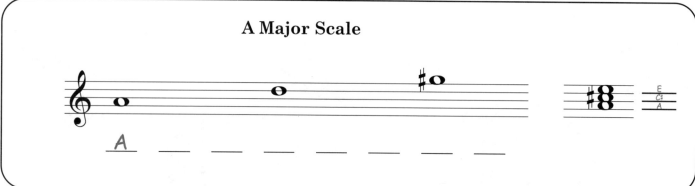

A ___ ___ ___ ___ ___ ___ ___

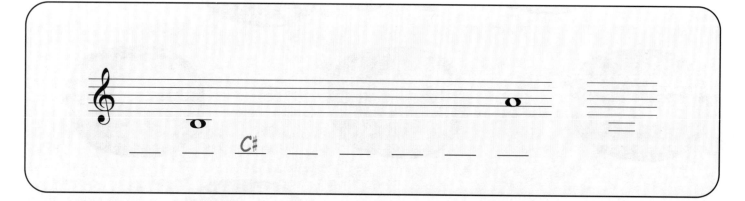

___ ___ C♯ ___ ___ ___ ___ ___

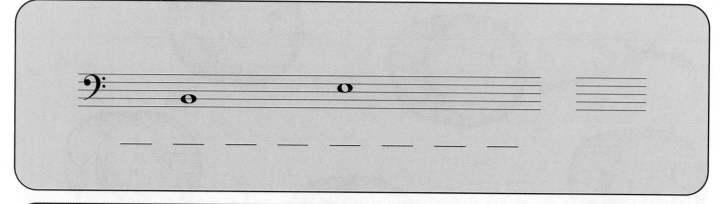

___ ___ ___ ___ ___ ___ ___ ___

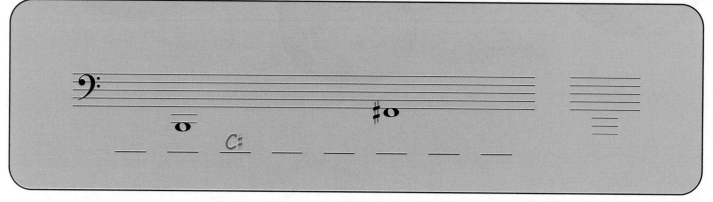

___ ___ C♯ ___ ___ ___ ___ ___

FJH2209

". . . Advancing to Black Belt"

· Draw the missing Major triad notes in each belt and name the notes.

Accidentals and Ledger Line Notes

"It's the Computer Age . . .

· Name the notes in each monitor. Play each note.

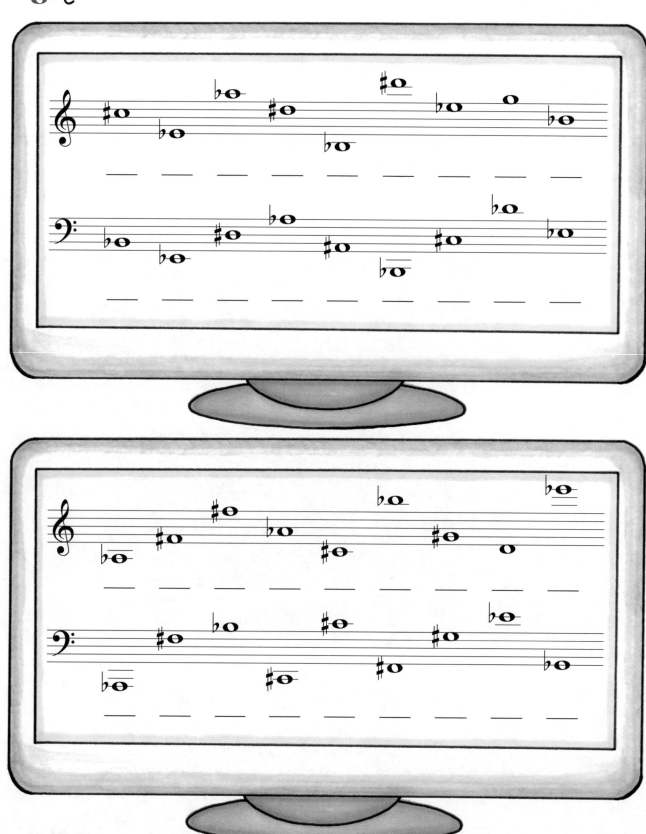

FJH2209

. . . with Cell Phones"

· Name the notes.

Accidentals and Ledger Line Notes

"School Days . . .

- Connect the correct answer to each bus window.

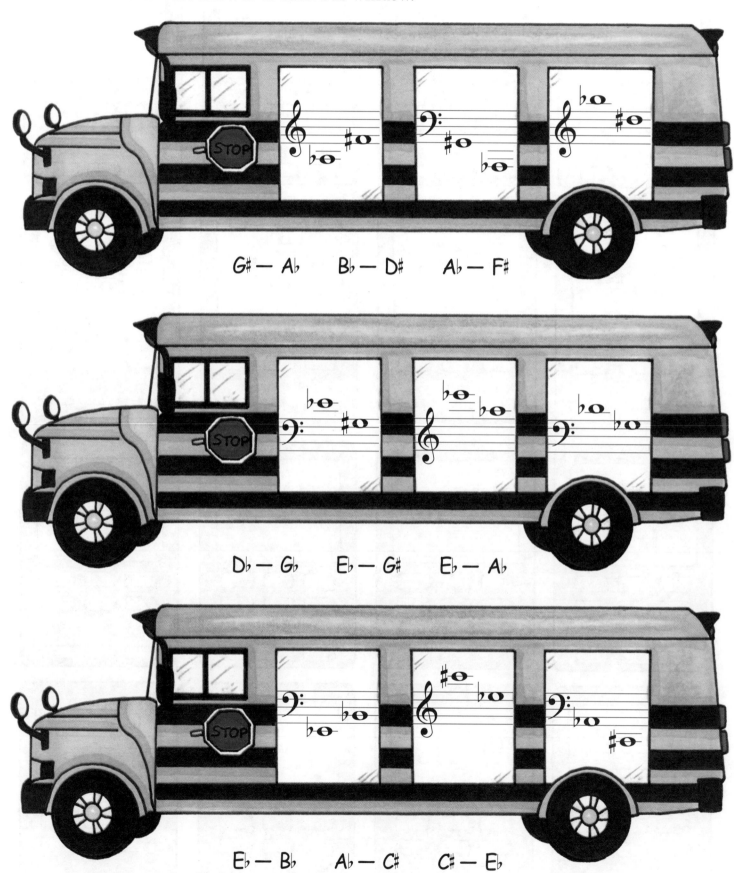

G♯ — A♭   B♭ — D♯   A♭ — F♯

D♭ — G♭   E♭ — G♯   E♭ — A♭

E♭ — B♭   A♭ — C♯   C♯ — E♭

. . . Reading, Writing Accidentals"

- Name each note and connect each school locker to the locker containing the enharmonic notes.

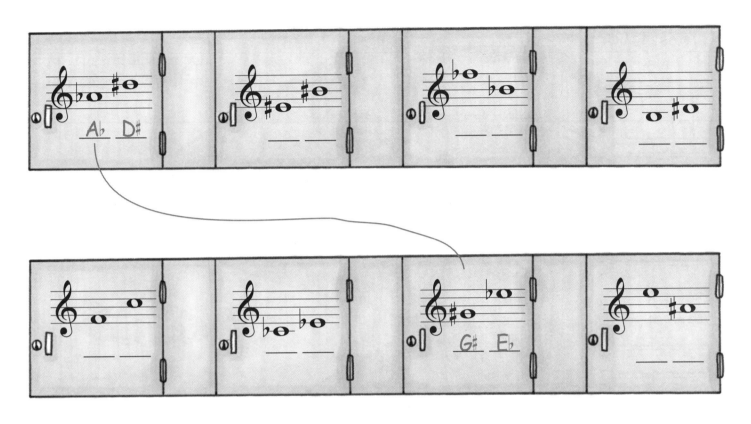

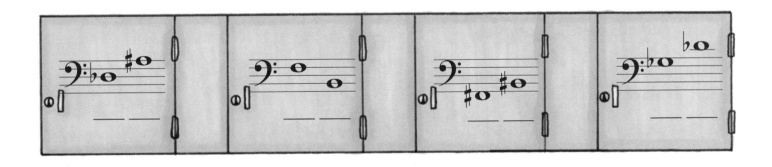

The F Major Scale

"School's Out . . .

F Major has
1♭ — B♭

- Fill in the missing notes of the F Major scale.

- Draw the missing notes of the F Major scale.

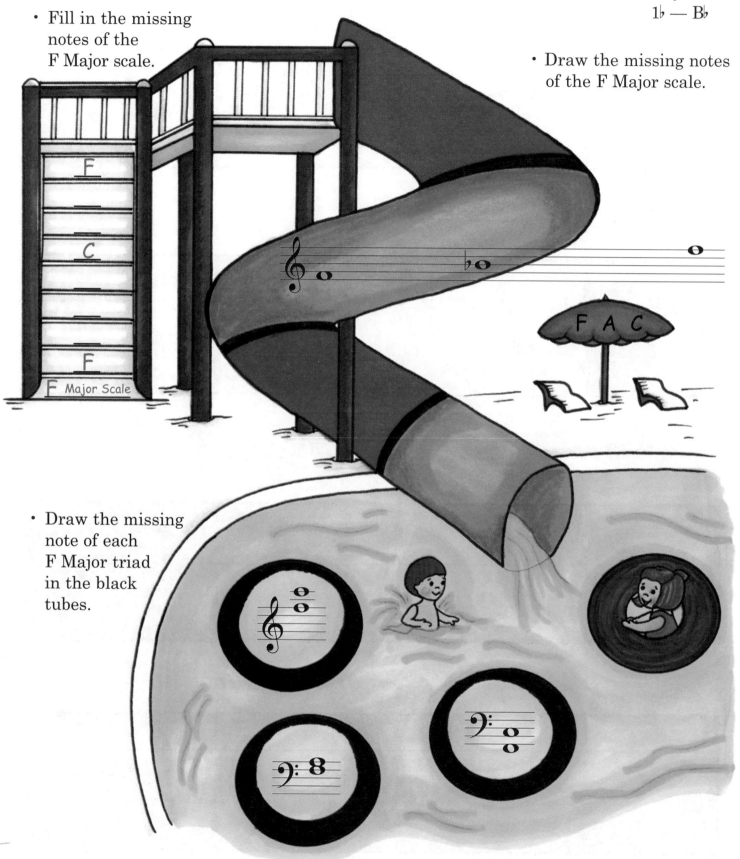

- Draw the missing note of each F Major triad in the black tubes.

FJH2209

... Let's Go to the Water Park"

- Fill in the missing notes of the F Major scale in the water slide.
- Draw and name the missing F Major triad notes in the water floats and black tubes.

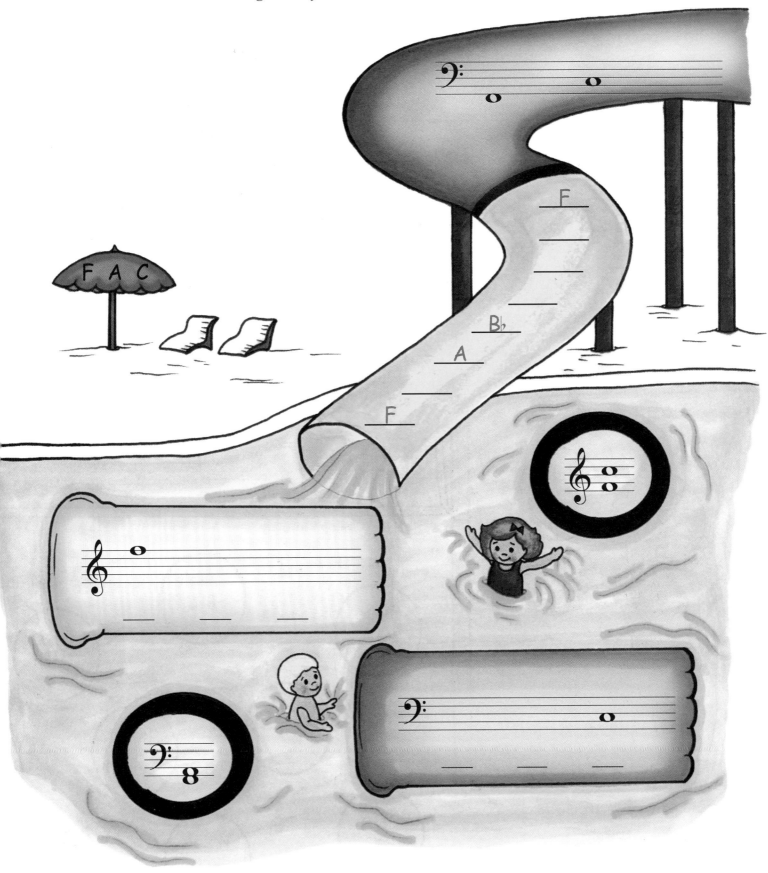

Notes and Harmonic Intervals
"More Summer Fun . . .

• Write the number beside the harmonic interval

FJH2209

. . . Playing Beach Volleyball"

in the correct volleyball on each page.

Certificate of Achievement

_____

Student

has completed

Succeeding with a Notespeller

GRADE 2B

Now you know all your notes!

T H E
F·J·H
MUSIC
COMPANY
I N C.

Frank J. Hackinson

_____   _____
Date   Teacher's Signature